AMISH
PRAYERS &
PROVERBS

Publications International, Ltd.

Fellowship and Blessings from Above

The best things in life are not things.

—Amish proverb

Fellowship is important in Amish culture, as is the weekly church service. The Amish gather on Sunday morning to greet each other with hearty handshakes and holy kisses. Children are active participants, though younger children will sometimes interrupt the service with their antics—much to everyone's delight.

After services, everyone stays for a fellowship meal. The meal may be simple, but the camaraderie and laughter are strong.

Many think the Amish, with their days filled with love and joy, lead idyllic lives. But the lives of the Amish aren't perfect. Theirs are filled with sorrows, illnesses, death, and struggles—just as ours are. But they know who to talk to when problems arise and who to thank for the good things they encounter.

Though most of us don't want to live without our conveniences and modern gadgets, we can still share in the wisdom of the Amish.

Let the joy, love, laughter, and community of the Amish be part of your life. We can keep our computers and high-definition TVs, but our lives could be improved if we learn some good sense from the Amish.

A heart touched by grace brings joy to the face.

The fear of the Lord is the beginning of knowledge: but fools despise wisdom and instruction.

—Proverbs 1:7

The person who forgives does more for himself than for anyone else.

We can stop forgiving others when Christ stops forgiving us.

Never doubt in the dark what God has shown you in the light.

You cannot change life—because God on high
controls this world with an all-seeing eye.
He makes the calls and you're never alone;
all's well in heaven and God's on the throne.

You can't stumble when you are on your knees.

Let your life story be for God's glory.

We are not promised skies always blue, but a Helper to see us through.

Bibles that are coming apart usually belong to people who are not.

If you want your life to be a reflection of Christ, you need to take time to reflect on Christ.

Train up a child in the way he should go: and when he is old, he will not depart from it.

—**Proverbs 22:6**

Before we can pray, "Thy Kingdom come," we must pray, "My kingdom go."

Live each short hour with God, and the long years will take care of themselves.

To mistreat God's creation is to offend the Creator.

Amish Table Prayer

*Enable us to use Thy manifold blessings
    with moderation;
Grant our hearts wisdom to avoid excess
    in eating and drinking
    and in the cares of this life;
Teach us to put our trust in Thee
    and to await Thy helping hand.*

*For the wisdom of this world is foolishness with God.
For it is written, He taketh the wise in their own
craftiness.*

—1 Corinthians 3:19

A faith worth having is a faith worth sharing.

God likes small people. He cannot use big ones.

Our duty is not to see through one another but to see one another through.

We are never worthless, but unworthy.

Only one life, 'twill soon be past;
only what's done for Christ will last.

Faith produces a way of life that pleases God.

Do unto others as if you were the other.

Trusting God turns problems into opportunities.

Doubt has never changed anything.
Belief changes things.

Faith gives us the courage to face the present with
confidence and the future with expectancy.

*After this manner therefore pray ye: Our Father which
art in heaven, Hallowed be thy name. Thy kingdom
come, Thy will be done in earth, as it is in heaven.
Give us this day our daily bread. And forgive us our
debts, as we forgive our debtors. And lead us not
into temptation, but deliver us from evil: For thine is
the kingdom, and the power, and the glory, for ever.
Amen.*

—**Matthew 6:9–13**

When I have nothing left but God,
then I find that God is all I need.

Kindness, when given away, keeps coming back.

Just because I cannot do everything does not give me the right to do nothing.

If you are true to your faith, there are things you give up for your faith.

It may be difficult to wait on the Lord,
but it is worse to wish you had.

You only live once, but if you work it right, once is enough.

If you sense your faith unraveling, go back to where you dropped the thread of obedience.

And be not conformed to this world: but be ye transformed by the renewing of your mind, that ye may prove what is that good, and acceptable, and perfect, will of God.

—**Romans 12:2**

Faith hears the inaudible, sees the invisible, believes the incredible, and receives the impossible.

He who bows lowest in the presence of God stands straightest in the presence of sin.

Let us not pray for lighter burdens but for stronger backs.

God has work for all his children, regardless of age or ability.

Walk softly, speak tenderly, and pray fervently.

Contentment and trust are characteristics of a sanctified life.

Enjoy today; it won't come back.

Every moment of worry weakens the soul for its daily combat.

Whoso rewardeth evil for good, evil shall not depart from his house.

—**Proverbs 17:13**

A happy life and eternal salvation
is spoiling the devil's calculation.

Wherever we go, God is there.
Whenever we call, God is listening.
Whatever we need, God is enough.

He that trusteth in his own heart is a fool:
but whoso walketh wisely, he shall be delivered.

—Proverbs 28:26

When you get to your wit's end, you'll find God lives there.

God's best is known by surrender—not struggle.

The higher a man gets in divine grace, the lower he will be in his own esteem.

The person who sows seeds of kindness will have a perpetual harvest.

The seed of discouragement will not grow in a thankful heart.

The best way to escape evil is to pursue good.

Don't pray when it rains if you don't pray when the sun shines.

To overcome sin, starve the old nature and feed the new.

Hope for the best, prepare for the worst, and take what comes with a smile.

God could save us from trauma, but instead he sends us a Comforter.

Generosity leaves a much better taste than stinginess.

Boast not thyself of to morrow; for thou knowest not what a day may bring forth.

—Proverbs 27:1

Happiness doesn't come from doing what we like to do, but liking what we have to do.

Faith is the bridge over which we can cross all the unknown waters of tomorrow.

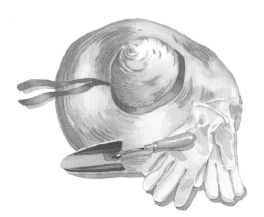

Humility comes from understanding that the obstacles in front of you will not go away.

A heart at peace gives life to the body.

A person who lives for himself never knows the real joys of life.

A heart at peace gives life to the body.

Be faithful, and leave the results to God.

It is easier to preach a sermon than to live one.

Never be afraid to do what is right, even if all the others are doing what is wrong.

Kind words and kind deeds
keep life's garden free of weeds.

We are known by our actual deeds and not by what we boast we can do.

God has two dwellings, one in heaven and the other in a meek and thankful heart.

Let not mercy and truth forsake thee: bind them about thy neck; write them upon the table of thine heart: So shalt thou find favour and good understanding in the sight of God and man.

—**Proverbs 3:3–4**

God won't lead you where his grace can't keep you.

It is better to hold out a helping hand than to point a finger.

When fear knocks at the door, send faith to answer!

If we live right each day, we need neither be afraid of tomorrow nor ashamed of yesterday.

Patience is a virtue that carries a lot of wait.

Know the Bible in your head,
stow it in your heart,
show it in your life,
sow it in the world.

Nothing lasts forever, not even your troubles.

Better to die honest than to live in disgrace.

He that gathereth in summer is a wise son: but he that sleepeth in harvest is a son that causeth shame.

—Proverbs 10:5

Those who let God provide will always be satisfied.

A man should not grieve overmuch, for that is a complaint against God.

Knowledge is the power of the mind.
Wisdom is the power of the soul.

When you find time on your hands, put them together in prayer.

The merciful man doeth good to his own soul:
but he that is cruel troubleth his own flesh.

—Proverbs 11:17

When you speak, always remember that God is one of your listeners.

The higher the mountain, the deeper the valley.

The smallest deed is better than the greatest intention.

We value the light more fully after we've come through the darkness.

A truly humble person is not easily offended.

The person who sows seeds of kindness will have a perpetual harvest.

God speaks to those who are quiet before him.

Love always finds a home in the heart of a friend.

Kind words can be short and easy to speak, but their echoes are truly endless.

A sound heart is the life of the flesh:
but envy the rottenness of the bones.

—Proverbs 14:30

We should not put a question mark where God puts a period.

Friendships cemented by sin do not hold.

A heart at peace gives life to the body.

The key to contentment is to realize that life is a gift—not a right.

Peace is rarely denied to the peaceful.

You cannot truly be a child of God without resembling the Father.

Love enables us to walk fearlessly, to run confidently, and to live victoriously.

Conscience: that still, small voice that makes you even smaller.

Develop a forgiving attitude.

Don't let anger fester for too long.
Make the first move toward reconciliation.

When pride cometh, then cometh shame:
but with the lowly is wisdom.

—**Proverbs 11:2**

The waves of hatred beat in vain against the rock of love.

What one does cheerfully is no burden.

Need teaches prayer.